Booker T. Washington

by Lola M. Schaefer

Consulting Editor: Gail Saunders-Smith, Ph.D.
Consultant: Horace Porter, Chair,
African American World Studies Department,
University of Iowa, Iowa City, Iowa

Pebble Books

an imprint of Capstone Press
Mankato, Minnesota

Pebble Books are published by Capstone Press
151 Good Counsel Drive, P.O. Box 669, Mankato, Minnesota 56002
http://www.capstone-press.com

1 2 3 4 5 6 08 07 06 05 04 03

Library of Congress Cataloging-in-Publication Data
Schaefer, Lola M., 1950–
    Booker T. Washington / by Lola M. Schaefer.
    p. cm.—(First biographies)
    Summary: Simple text and photographs introduce the life of
Booker T. Washington.
    Includes bibliographical references (p. 23) and index.
    ISBN 0-7368-1647-X (hardcover)
    1. Washington, Booker T., 1856–1915—Juvenile literature. 2. African
Americans—Biography—Juvenile literature. 3. Educators—United States—
Biography—Juvenile literature. [1. Washington, Booker T., 1856–1915.
2. Educators. 3. African Americans—Biography.] I. Title. II. First biographies
(Mankato, Minn.)
E185.97.W4 S23 2003
370′.92—dc21   2002011746

Note to Parents and Teachers

The First Biographies series supports national history standards for
units on people and culture. This book describes and illustrates the
life of Booker T. Washington. The photographs support early readers
in understanding the text. This book also introduces early readers to
subject-specific vocabulary words, which are defined in the Words
to Know section. Early readers may need assistance to read some
words and to use the Table of Contents, Words to Know, Read More,
Internet Sites, and Index/Word List sections of the book.

Table of Contents

Time Line

1856
born

4

Booker was born in Virginia in 1856. He did not have a last name because he was a slave.

slaves working in cotton field

Time Line

1856 1865
born moves to
West Virginia

Booker and his family became free in 1865. They moved to West Virginia. Booker went to work in a salt mine.

salt miners working at a coastal mine

Time Line

1856　1865
born　moves to
West Virginia

8

Booker wanted to go to school. He learned to read the numbers on the salt barrels. He learned the alphabet from a book his mother gave him.

young Booker

Time Line

1856
born

1865
moves to
West Virginia

1872
enrolls at
Hampton Institute

Booker needed a last name at school. He chose the name Washington. In 1872, he enrolled at Hampton Institute. It was a school for African Americans.

Hampton Institute in the late 1800s

Time Line

1856
born

1865
moves to
West Virginia

1872
enrolls at
Hampton Institute

Booker worked as a janitor to help pay for school. He learned reading, writing, and math. He also learned to farm and to lay bricks.

Time Line

1856
born

14

1865
moves to
West Virginia

1872
enrolls at
Hampton Institute

1875
graduates from
Hampton Instit

In 1875, Booker graduated from Hampton Institute. He became a teacher. In 1881, he opened a new school. He called this school Tuskegee.

◀ Booker riding his horse on the Tuskegee grounds

1881
opens
Tuskegee

Time Line

1856	1865	1872	1875
born	moves to West Virginia	enrolls at Hampton Institute	graduates from Hampton Institu

Booker wanted Tuskegee students to learn reading, writing, history, and science. He also wanted them to learn a trade.

◄ Tuskegee students working in an electrical shop

Time Line

1856	1865	1872	1875
born	moves to	enrolls at	graduates from
	West Virginia	Hampton Institute	Hampton Instit

18

In 1895, Booker gave a speech in Atlanta, Georgia. He asked African Americans to learn useful trades and earn their rights as Americans.

Booker speaking to a crowd

1881
opens
Tuskegee

1895
gives speech
in Atlanta

Time Line

1856
born

1865
moves to
West Virginia

1872
enrolls at
Hampton Institute

1875
graduates from
Hampton Institu

In 1901, Booker published his life story. He called his book *Up From Slavery*. He was a leader of African Americans until his death in 1915.

1881
opens
Tuskegee

1895
gives speech
in Atlanta

1901
publishes *Up
From Slavery*

1915
dies

Words to Know

African American—a citizen of the United States with an African background

alphabet—all the letters of a language

earn—to work to get a result

enroll—to begin studies at a school

graduate—to finish studies at a school and receive a diploma

janitor—someone whose job is to look after and clean a school or other building

mine—an underground supply of minerals, metals, coal, or salt

publish—to make and distribute a book, magazine, or newspaper so that people can buy it and read it

slave—a person owned by another person; slaves were not free to choose their homes or jobs.

trade—a job or craft

Read More

Gosda, Randy T. *Booker T. Washington: A Buddy Book*. First Biographies. Edina, Minn.: Abdo Publishing, 2002.

McKissack, Pat, and Frederick McKissack. *Booker T. Washington: Leader and Educator*. Great African Americans. Berkeley Heights, N.J.: Enslow Publishers, 2001.

Troy, Don. *Booker T. Washington*. Journey to Freedom. Chanhassen, Minn.: Child's World, 1999.

Internet Sites

Track down many sites about Booker T. Washington. Visit the FACT HOUND at *http://www.facthound.com*

IT IS EASY! IT IS FUN!

1) Go to *http://www.facthound.com*

2) Type in: 073681647X

3) Click on "FETCH IT" and FACT HOUND will find several links hand-picked by our editors.

Relax and let our pal FACT HOUND do the research for you!

Index/Word List

Word Count: 209
Early-Intervention Level: 18

Editorial Credits
Jennifer VanVoorst, editor; Heather Kindseth, cover designer and illustrator;
    Juliette Peters, production designer; Linda Clavel, illustrator; Karrey Tweten,
    photo researcher

Photo Credits
Corbis, 1, 12, 16; Bettmann, 4; Francis Benjamin Johnson, 14
Getty Images/Hulton Archive, cover, 6, 20
Hampton University, 10
Library of Congress, 18
UNC at Chapel Hill Rare Book Collection, 8